W9-CAR-438

Wild Science Careers

FORENSIC SCIENTIST

Careers Solving Crimes and Scientific Mysteries

JUDITH WILLIAMS

Enslow Publishers, Inc.
40 Industrial Road
Box 398
Berkeley Heights, NJ 07922
USA

http://www.enslow.com

For Patricia—Forensic Fan and Friend Extraordinaire

Acknowledgments

The author would like to thank Heidi Robbins, Sam Andrews, Gail Anderson, Ed Espinoza, Elizabeth Rega, and Alison Galloway for their generous effort, time, and contributions in this project. Thanks also for the assistance of the U.S. Fish and Wildlife Service Forensic Laboratory; the Office of the Chief Medical Examiner, Calgary, Alberta; and Nikola Korniyuk and the Victoria Experimental Network Under the Sea, Victoria, British Columbia.

Library of Congress Cataloging-in-Publication Data

Williams, Judith (Judith A.)
    Forensic scientist : careers solving crimes and scientific mysteries / by Judith Williams.
      p. cm. — (Wild science careers)
    Summary: "Explores the science of and careers in forensics using several examples of real-life scientists"—Provided by publisher.
    Includes bibliographical references and index.
    ISBN-13: 978-0-7660-3051-0
    ISBN-10: 0-7660-3051-2
    1. Forensic sciences—Vocational guidance—Juvenile literature. 2. Forensic scientists—Vocational guidance—Juvenile literature. I. Title.
    HV8073.8.W545 2009
    363.25023—dc22   2008004680

Printed in the United States of America

10 9 8 7 6 5 4 3 2 1

To Our Readers: We have done our best to make sure all Internet Addresses in this book were active and appropriate when we went to press. However, the author and the publisher have no control over and assume no liability for the material available on those Internet sites or on other Web sites they may link to. Any comments or suggestions can be sent by e-mail to comments@enslow.com or to the address on the back cover.

♻ Enslow Publishers, Inc., is committed to printing our books on recycled paper. The paper in every book contains 10% to 30% post-consumer waste (PCW). The cover board on the outside of each book contains 100% PCW. Our goal is to do our part to help young people and the environment too!

Photo Credits: Courtesy of Alison Galloway, p. 100; Courtesy of David Pursley, p. 96; Courtesy of Elizabeth Rega, pp. 83, 90, 92; Courtesy of the Los Angeles County Sheriff's Office Crime Lab, pp. 5, 11, 16, 19; Courtesy of the Office of the Chief Medical Examiner, Calgary, Alberta, pp. 24, 33, 34; Courtesy of r.r. jones and the University of California at Santa Cruz, p. 97; Courtesy of Simon Fraser University, p. 44; Courtesy of U.S. Fish and Wildlife Forensics Laboratory, pp. 62, 64, 67, 68; Courtesy of VENUS Project/University of Victoria, pp. 58, 59; Courtesy of Western University of Health Sciences, p. 79; © Enslow Publishers, Inc., p. 65; Jim Kondrat, Paleo-Tech Concepts, p. 104; © Kim Taylor/npl/Minden Pictures, pp. 43, 47; © Lawrence Sawyer/iStockphoto.com, p. 78; © Matthias Breiter/Minden Pictures, p. 61; Mauro Fermariello/Photo Researchers, Inc., p. 30; © Michael W. Skrepnick, p. 81; Shutterstock, pp. 1, 4, 23, 112; © Warwick Sloss/npl/Minden Pictures, p. 51.

Cover Photo: AFP/Getty Images

Contents

CHAPTER 1

The Calling Card Murderer

Criminalist Heidi Robbins sorts through the bags and bags of evidence. She spreads out the crime scene photographs. As she reads the case report, her eyes flicker back to the photographs and evidence before her. She pays careful attention to the details as a story of violence and murder unfolds....

A career as a criminalist is one of many paths in the dynamic field of forensic science. **Forensics** uses science to help law enforcement solve and prove crimes. Depictions of forensic science are everywhere—in television, films, and even games at the toy store—but these are often fictional, glossing over the gritty reality of the profession. In real life, obtaining **DNA** results can take weeks. Scientists do not chase

Heidi Robbins is a senior criminalist and the assistant director of the Scientific Services Bureau Crime Lab at the Los Angeles County Sheriff's Department.

suspects down alleys with firearms drawn, either. Most criminalists do not carry weapons, even in major cities like Los Angeles. The stories played out on television have little in common with the day-to-day activities of the men and women who pursue forensics as a career.

While solving **homicides** to keep society safe is important, forensics is not always about crime. Sometimes it involves discovering clues to events so old that the victim died a hundred years ago, or even millions of years ago. But whatever scientific trail leads to a career in forensics, the fascination is the same—using science to solve a mystery.

A Body in the Dumpster

The criminalist and forensic identification specialist (FIS) arrive at the scene in separate vehicles. They see uniformed officers and detectives in the area of the Dumpster. The criminalist takes her crime scene kit and the FIS brings his camera, stopping to speak to the detectives who called them to the homicide scene.

In a crime lab team as large as this one, there are often specialists for each kind of evidence collection. Usually the FIS is called in to document the crime scene. The detectives call in for help from a criminalist as well if there is a lot of evidence to be processed, particularly if there is blood on the scene. Tonight, both the FIS and the criminalist are required.[1]

Investigating the Scene

As the people from the crime lab approach the Dumpster, they look around carefully. Their eyes survey the area for evidence left behind. At the same time, they glance up and down the alley for people who might be hiding. Although the officers have secured the area, it would not be the first time that a suspect returned to a crime scene. Criminalists are not police officers and do not carry weapons. Even driving to crime scenes can be dangerous in crime-ridden parts of a city. Danger is part of the job, and tonight, the forensics specialists proceed with care.

Any object near the crime scene that could be evidence is examined. Then the forensics team begins its analysis of the Dumpster. The FIS takes photos of the crime scene from different angles. The next step is to look for fingerprints. On a Dumpster there could be lots of them from many different people. The FIS is also a latent print examiner, a specialist in the collection of finger, palm, and footprints.[2] To collect the fingerprints, he first dusts them with powder and then puts transparent tape over them to "lift" the print off the surface of the Dumpster. Each print is photographed at the same time. Then the tape is carefully removed and attached to a fingerprint card. Cards and photos are all documented as evidence. It is possible that none of the prints are related to the crime, but the FIS must collect them to be sure.

The criminalist is in charge of gathering the remaining forensic evidence. She takes note of where the body lies in the Dumpster. The **decedent** is covered with blankets and several other objects. Among these is a large black rubber liner from the bed of a pickup truck. The liner helped hide the body from view, possibly the plan of the person who put the body there.

Inside the Dumpster

Investigating a Dumpster is a challenge—and this Dumpster is a large one. As crime scenes go, this is a smelly and dirty location. Confronted with bags and bags of garbage, it is difficult to know what might be important evidence and what is not. The criminalist puts on a jumpsuit before investigating dirty crime scenes, whether it is to crawl underneath a vehicle, visit an **arson** scene, or climb into a Dumpster.

She pulls on gloves to protect her hands from the victim's **biological fluids**. The gloves and jumpsuit also prevent the criminalist from accidentally leaving fingerprints or hairs of her own as "evidence" on the crime scene.

A quick look at the scene reveals something dark over some of the contents of the Dumpster. The criminalist applies a chemical from a small bottle to the dark spots. This test confirms that the spots are blood. The forensics team must go through the evidence piece by piece. They are searching for any clue that might quickly give them information about possible suspects. Once they return to the crime lab, they will carefully inspect each piece of evidence again.

The FIS and the criminalist next examine the items closest to the body. In this case, the victim has several things stacked on top of her. They pull out the heavy black rubber pickup truck bed liner. There are indentations on it where it fit over the wheel wells of the truck. That might help match the liner to a truck later in the case. Most importantly, the rubber liner has blood on it, probably linking it to the homicide victim. Every object collected is photographed.

The criminalist pulls several blankets off the decedent. The blankets have bloodstains on them.

One heavy wool blanket even has a bloody footwear impression on it. The criminalist is happy to find that, as it is potentially a solid clue that could lead to potential suspects.

She also removes a large piece of carpet from the Dumpster. There is a bloodstain on it. In addition, the carpet has a jagged edge, showing that it has been cut or torn.

The team recovers a wrapped-up, bloody towel next. They are curious because there is some kind of food inside the towel. The food is white and chopped up in small bits.

One Small Card Is One Big Piece of Evidence

The Dumpster's next best clue is revealed when the team pulls out several pieces of paper. One of them is a business card advertising a tire retreading business.

This small business card carries important evidence. First, one third of it is soaked in blood, probably the victim's. Second, the back of the card carries the impression of a partial boot print. Three **lug** marks left a distinctive pattern. (Lugs are the raised part of a sole that gives traction to a boot.)

Working carefully, the team removes the body from

the Dumpster. The victim endured many injuries, including cutting wounds to her right hand. People who work in forensics call these defensive wounds. Usually they are caused when victims try to defend themselves from an attack.

Staff from the medical examiner's office arrives to take the body to the morgue, where the staff will work to identify the body and determine the cause of

This business card was found at the scene of a crime with a bloody boot print on it.

death. Meanwhile, detectives are looking for witnesses and speaking to people nearby who may have information about the crime. The forensics team shows the detectives the business card. The detectives realize from looking at the address that the tire retreading business is in the neighborhood.

The detectives and forensics team believe the suspect dumped everything out of his truck that was related to the homicide, including the bed liner. Given the blood evidence and the business card, the detectives request a search warrant for the tire business. A search warrant will give the detectives permission to search the tire business and its owner for more clues. If the detectives find objects that might help prove their case, they can legally take them as evidence.

Meanwhile, the forensics team returns to collecting and documenting evidence about the crime. The criminalist must decide which of the objects they have found might be important to the investigation and which are not.

Tools for Evidence Collection

Kits for gathering evidence are quite simple. They contain gloves, bags, rulers, notepaper, and swabs.

Forceps are used for picking up smaller objects or things that should not be touched, such as the blood-soaked business card. Much of the evidence is collected and stored in paper bags of varying sizes. All evidence is numbered and recorded.

Evidence must be carefully stored so that it will not be lost. Biological evidence such as blood, saliva, and sweat must be placed in a container that will allow it to dry out properly, such as one made of paper. Usually, such items are placed in paper bags. Once this evidence is dry, it is frozen for later study. Larger objects, such as the carpet piece, are placed in cardboard boxes that allow the biological evidence to dry out. Items that are not biological, such as **accelerants**, are placed in airtight containers.

Trace Evidence

Small items—such as powders, fibers, glass fragments, hair, and paint chips—are called trace evidence. They are collected in envelopes or **bindles** for safekeeping. A bindle, also known as a druggist's fold, is an effective but low-tech way of collecting evidence. Forensic scientists fold paper in several directions to hold trace evidence securely. They are limited only by the size of paper they have in their kits. The bindles and envelopes are placed in boxes for storage.

At the Los Angeles County Sheriff's Crime Lab, says Robbins, footprints are considered impression evidence. They are examined in the trace laboratory. Tire tracks and footwear impressions are photographed by the FIS.

The Case Continues

The forensics team transports the remaining evidence to the crime lab for further analysis. The detectives get the search warrant they need for the address on the bloodstained business card. Meanwhile, the body found in the Dumpster is identified from her fingerprints. Once this is done, her family is notified.

Outside the tire retreading business, the detectives spot a pickup truck. A close examination of it shows that it recently had a liner that was removed. They can tell by the distance of the wheel wells that the indentations in the liner found in the Dumpster would match perfectly, and would fit the same model of truck. Inspecting the truck, they see bloodstains down the back bumper. The detectives see that the forensics team must be called to collect evidence from this potential crime scene, too.

At the Original Scene of the Crime

Once inside the tire business, the first thing the detectives and the criminalist see is a bloody footwear impression. Its markings match the pattern on the blanket recovered from the Dumpster. The lab will need to compare the two impressions to be certain. If they match—and they seem to—the criminalists can link that footwear impression to the one found with the body.

The impression is an important part of solving this crime, but only if the detectives can recover footwear that matches. The suspect from the tire shop lives at the same location, and leather boots with a matching tread are easily found. An examination of the boots shows blood on both the sides and the soles.

When the criminalists look in the tire shop, they find spots of blood. Robbins says the blood pattern is "consistent with a stabbing."

The next evidence the criminalist finds is a piece of carpet. Like the carpet found in the Dumpster, this one is also bloodstained. The carpet has a jagged tear. Later, when the piece of carpet found in the tire business is laid next to the one found in the Dumpster, the carpet pieces fit together perfectly, like pieces in a jigsaw puzzle. The final piece of evidence is located in the garbage, a container with chopped white food inside it. Later analysis will match it to the food in the towel uncovered in the Dumpster: cole slaw.

The forensics team collects the boots and the carpet, as well as blood evidence and photographs of the scene. They are now ready to transport all of the evidence to the crime lab for further analysis.

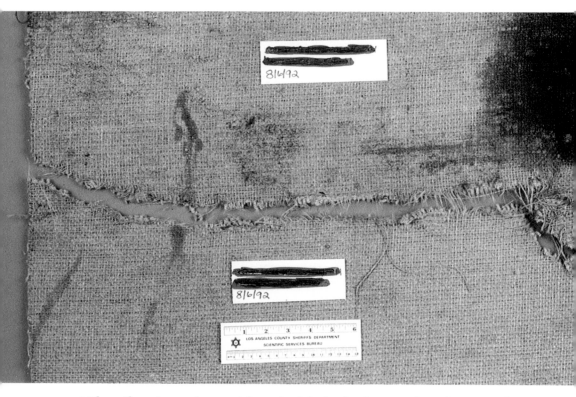

When the piece of carpet found with the body was placed next to the jagged carpet at the suspect's shop, the edges matched perfectly.

At the Crime Lab— Blood Analysis

Robbins is responsible for all the blood analyses on this case. She performs tests that make the blood proteins stand out. Knowing which types of proteins are present in the blood helps Robbins narrow down potential blood matches.

Now, instead of typing proteins, crime labs type DNA—the material inside cells that holds a person's genetic code. This code determines what makes each individual unique. DNA analysis is helpful for crime labs because DNA can be tested from blood, saliva, hair, and other parts of the body. But testing takes time. At the L.A. County Sheriff's Crime Lab, DNA analysis takes about six weeks.

When the tests from this case are complete, Robbins is able to match the blood on the towel, carpet, blanket, boots, truck, and the scene at the tire shop to the stabbing victim. That blood trail leads directly to the suspect.

Trace Evidence: The Boots

When Robbins is finished with the blood analysis of the leather boots, she passes them on to someone in the lab who specializes in trace evidence. This senior criminalist does the footwear imprint comparisons on this case. She compares the imprints from the carpet and blanket, matching the tread pattern to the suspect's leather boots. Then she analyzes the three lug marks on the business card. Using a **stereomicroscope**, the criminalist discovers that the three lugs on

The blood and distinctive lug pattern on the bottom of this boot helped bring a criminal to justice. The red arrows show places where Robbins tested for blood evidence.

the boots have unique characteristics. Identical marks are stained in blood on the business card. This proves that "those boots, and only those boots, made the marks on the business card."

Preparing Evidence for Court

All collecting, storing, documenting, and analyzing of evidence must be done properly, or the courts will not accept it. Once in court, any evidence can be challenged. To prevent this, standards used by the criminalists and everyone within the lab are strict. According to Robbins, "Forensic scientists undergo extensive training to ensure that they understand the methods [for handling and testing evidence] and the conclusions that can be reached."

One final step is taken to ensure the quality of evidence within the lab. All case work is reviewed by at least one other criminalist. With these procedures in place, all aspects of law enforcement can be sure that any evidence presented in court will be of the highest quality.

Testifying in Court

The final job for the criminalist is to prepare for testifying in court. Robbins reviews all the materials associated with the case as sometimes a long time passes before a case goes to trial. Her review includes all photographs, notes, and reports. As she reads everything over, she writes down the important details to remind herself of the different aspects of the case. Being able to confidently recall details in court helps a criminalist appear knowledgeable about the evidence. Now that Robbins has testified in court many times, it is much easier for her.

She explains how she handles appearing in court. "I used to be very uncomfortable speaking in front of people, which included juries. I used to get so nervous that I could hardly think on my feet. I found that if I memorized my court qualifications, one of the first questions you get asked, I could easily and smoothly recite them, which gave me confidence to move forward. I can't say I get nervous anymore, but the ability to be comfortable at public speaking is a skill that can be developed."

Giving successful testimony in court is just one part of the many duties required to be a criminalist. The blood analysis and the evidence of the partial boot print on the card are good examples of the attention to detail that is critical to a career in forensic science.

In the end, this case was cracked because of the combined efforts of the crime lab team, those who

A COOL GADGET: STEREOMICROSCOPE

Microscopes are essential to forensic work. An optical microscope allows tiny samples to be viewed. A stereomicroscope has two different features: it gives a 3-D image of evidence, and also allows larger items to be magnified and viewed. Newer stereomicroscopes display images on a monitor.

went to the scene, and the criminalists who did the analyses at the lab. With such powerful evidence, the detectives built a successful case, and the criminal was convicted for his crime.

A Career as a Criminalist

Although in the past many criminalists did not have a science degree, most crime labs now require one. Many criminalists obtain graduate degrees as well. Students who want to pursue a career as a criminalist should be strong in such subjects as chemistry and math. Once working in crime labs, criminalists will continue to study to keep their skills and knowledge up-to-date.

Working as a criminalist is interesting and challenging every day. Robbins says, "The best part of my job is being able to perform analyses which provide information to the detectives that answer questions toward solving the crime. Knowing that the work you did might prevent others from getting hurt is the most satisfying part of this job."

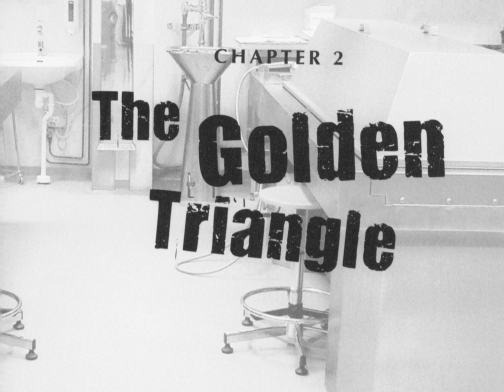

CHAPTER 2

The Golden Triangle

Albuquerque, New Mexico: Sam Andrews takes note of the body lying on the **autopsy** table. Accompanying it are two New Mexico police detectives who came to see the autopsy performed. Andrews is a forensic pathologist. His job is to explain sudden and unexpected death. This case qualifies. Usually police officers are not present for

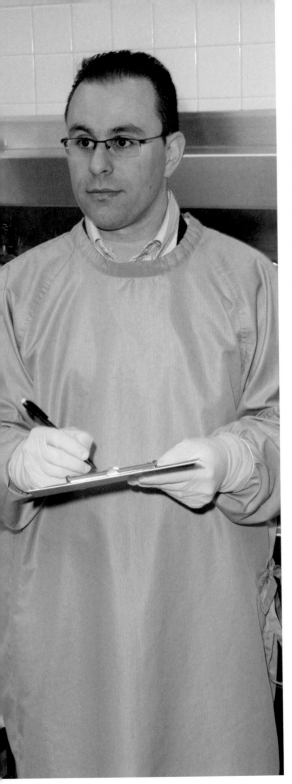

autopsies unless a death is considered suspicious. The detectives flip through their notes as they describe how the body was discovered.

Neighbors and the landlord called the police when they realized that a young woman in their building had not been seen for several days. Everyone was accustomed to seeing the young woman come and go regularly as she attended the local college. She was also known to be health-conscious and went running daily. As she lived alone, the young woman's sudden disappearance had

Dr. Sam Andrews is now the forensic pathologist and assistant chief medical examiner in Calgary, Alberta, Canada.

everyone concerned. The police were called to check her apartment to make sure she was all right.

The landlord opened the locked apartment for the police. The rooms showed evidence of the usual life of a busy college student: clothes everywhere, a computer, textbooks, and papers on her desk. There was no sign of the young woman, but the police noted that the bathroom door was closed and locked. They forced the door open and found that the concern of the neighbors had been justified. The college student was dead.

A Crime Scene?

Ordinarily, if the police find someone dead in a locked apartment and then a locked bathroom as well, they would assume that no one else was involved in the death. In this case, the detectives noticed that the bathroom window was wide open. The window was quite large, so it was possible that someone had harmed the young woman and then escaped that way instead of using the door.

Since the window had been left open, the bathroom was cold. In fact, the entire apartment was chilled to about 13°C (56°F). Although the woman was last seen six days before, no one knew when she actually had died. A cold room can slow down how a body **decomposes**, or decays.

The bathroom was messy, but there were clues that this was not just an untidy room. Wet clothes lay on the floor and in the shower. The towel and toilet paper racks were both torn off the walls. And by the window, brown-red streaks that looked like finger marks marred the white walls. Something unusual had definitely happened in this room.

The detectives then directed their investigation to the woman's body. Her legs were in the shower while the rest of her body lay on the floor. Much of her skin was an unusual brown-red color and looked like leather.

How the victim died is unknown. Now Sam Andrews will add his examination to the evidence. As a forensic pathologist, Andrews does this with the autopsy.

Preparing for the Autopsy

Andrews begins an autopsy by first considering the background information he has from the police. He sometimes goes to the scene of unexpected death himself, or he sends medical investigators who represent him to gather information from the scene. In this case, the detectives give him all the information they have. Meanwhile, the morgue technician prepares the body for the autopsy. In every autopsy, the body is treated with respect.

Andrews needs a medical history. Right now, the only background he has is that the decedent appears to have been a healthy, fit young woman. He takes a quick look at the body, noting the leathery, brown-red skin that the police reported. It looks like a bad chemical burn. Andrews finds it curious because this is not the kind of injury people normally get in their homes.

Clues from the Medical History

Medical investigators in Andrews' office contact the decedent's family to find out if she had any medical conditions that may have played a role in her death. The family reports that a year earlier the victim had been treated in the hospital after having a seizure. During a seizure, the brain's electrical activity changes. This can cause the body to do different things, including shaking or losing consciousness. Many different medical conditions can cause a seizure. In the case of the college student, the hospital determined the seizure had happened because she had drunk too much water.

We often hear that it is healthy to drink lots of water. However, like most things, too much is not only unhealthy, it can cause illness—even death. The human body requires the elements of its blood to be in balance. With the young woman, drinking excess water made the salt levels in her blood drop too much, causing a seizure.

Before he starts an autopsy, Andrews tries to form a list of possible causes of death. He puts all the facts together that he has learned so far: the scene the police reported, the victim's medical history, and the possible chemical burns on her skin. Andrews has a theory, but the autopsy will give him more information to discover if he is right.

Gear for the Job

Everyone working on the body uses protective gear during the autopsy. "We practice universal precautions—a mask, gloves and gowns—so we're not really at any more risk than someone at the hospital dealing with a live patient. We deal with a lot of individuals who abuse drugs and/or alcohol. They're a population that has a higher number of infectious or transmissible diseases. You could say we're at higher risk because of the population we serve, but it's not any different than if they were at the hospital. Cutting ourselves is a big thing. [But our gear keeps us] pretty safe."[1]

A camera is always used to document autopsies. Photos may be taken by the forensic pathologist, the morgue technician, or a medical photographer if one is on staff. Many photos are required if the autopsy is for a homicide investigation.

The External Examination

The first step in the autopsy is the external examination. Andrews explains that he does "a head-to-toe examination, looking for normal things that I would notice if I saw the decedent walking down the street." He notes everything about the person's appearance, including height and weight; hair, eye, and skin color; and any clothes and jewelry. Once this is done, the clothes and jewelry are removed and cataloged. Next, Andrews looks for marks on the body such as scars, tattoos, or evidence of previous surgery, which are noted if present.

The second stage of the examination is to check for injuries. In the case of the college student, other than the condition of her skin, there are no signs of injuries. Most of the time during autopsies there are

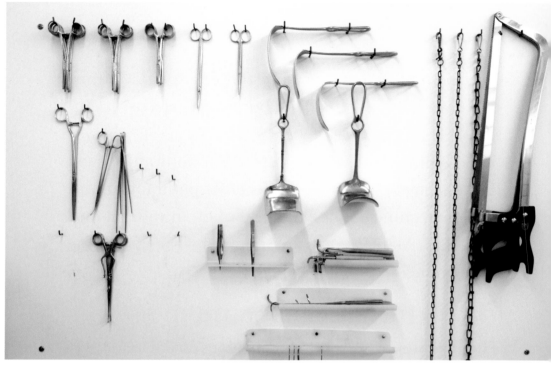

Many different instruments are used during an autopsy—including scalpels, scissors, tweezers, and bone saws!

no injuries present. Part of the reason for this is that 60 percent of all cases Andrews investigates are due to natural death, not homicide. This is typical for many places in North America other than the really large cities.

In homicide investigations, documenting injuries like gunshots or stabbings is very important. Andrews must note their location on the body, their size, direction, and how they look. With gunshot wounds, he tries to determine the distance from which the weapon was fired. The forensic pathologist's task is to discover the cause of death, and in a homicide weapons are usually the reason. Because of this, Andrews says the external examination is the most important part of an autopsy in a homicide investigation.

If the decedent was shot or stabbed, Andrews takes an X-ray. Sometimes a knife tip will break off and stay inside the body. An X-ray allows him to locate the knife tip or bullet, remove it, and then keep it as evidence.

The Investigation Moves Inside

The next step is the internal examination. Andrews is assisted by the morgue technician. Either the technician or the forensic pathologist makes the cut for the internal exam. Using a scalpel, the technician draws

A COOL GADGET:
CUT PROOF GLOVES

Cut proof gloves are made of a material similar to that used in modern body armor. These tough gloves prevent Andrews from accidentally cutting himself during an autopsy. He wears latex gloves, then the cut-proof gloves, and then another pair of latex gloves on top.

the blade down the body, making a cut in the shape of the letter Y. From each shoulder, a cut is made to the middle of the chest, forming the V of the Y. Where the two cuts meet, another one is made straight down to the pelvis. The skin is pulled back, revealing the tough chest plate of sternum and ribs. The plate protects the chest organs, and Andrews cannot see inside the chest cavity unless it is removed. To get inside, the technician cuts through the ribs using garden shears.

Once the chest plate is removed, Andrews looks inside the body for any sign of blood that does not belong there. Then the organs are removed. Different pathologists have different methods for organ removal. Some remove all the organs at one time. Others remove them in groups by how the organs function: for example, heart and lungs together. Andrews usually removes them one at a time. Each organ is weighed, and this information is written down on a form. Using scissors and forceps, he examines and then cuts into each organ using a long knife. To retrieve the brain, a special saw is used to cut the skull. It is the same kind that cuts casts off when patients have healed after breaking bones.

Andrews dissects the organs to look for any signs of injuries or disease that might be clues to the

The weight of each organ must be carefully recorded.

decedent's cause of death. After dissecting all the young woman's organs, Andrews concludes that they are normal.

Testing for Invisible Cause of Death

Sometimes the organs are diseased, but the evidence is invisible to the unaided eye. To check for possible diseases, Andrews prepares a tissue sample on a slide and views it using a microscope. Abnormal tissue will indicate a disease. All tissue is normal in this case.

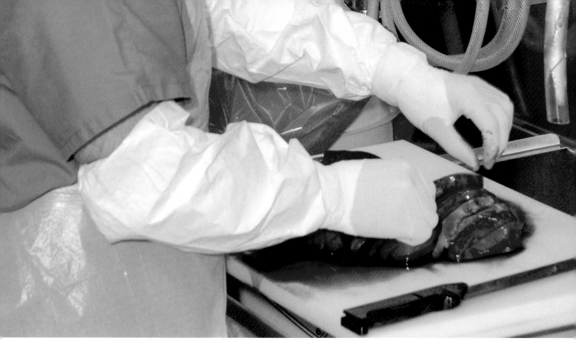

Dr. Andrews examines a human liver to look for signs of damage or disease.

When the examination of the organs is finished, they are placed back inside the body, the chest plate is returned to its place, and the body is sewed back up.

Testing blood is another way to find proof of disease. It is also used for the most common test done in the medical examiner's office—the **toxicology** test. This test shows the presence and quantity of drugs and alcohol in the body at the time of death. Given the healthy lifestyle of the college student, Andrews does not expect to find evidence of drugs or alcohol, but he tests for them anyway.

Returning to the Medical History

Since the examination of the body does not reveal an obvious cause of death, Andrews returns to the medical history of the victim. She was previously hospitalized because of a seizure. Unfortunately, evidence of a seizure will not usually show up in an autopsy examination. However, the reason for the young woman's seizure was documented. It occurred because of low salt levels from drinking too much water.

The forensic pathologist wants to test the salt levels in her body. When the patient was tested for this in the hospital, a blood test was used. After death, the best way to test salt levels is through removing fluid from the eye. To do this, Andrews uses a needle to remove the fluid. Both the eye fluid and the toxicology test blood sample are sent to a lab to be analyzed.

WILL A BODY BLEED DURING AN AUTOPSY?

No, because there is no blood pressure. Blood may leak out when blood vessels are cut, however. Autopsies are performed on tables that will drain the blood away from the body.

Because the victim appears to have a chemical burn, Andrews takes samples of the brown-red skin. Looking at the tissue under a microscope, he sees the signs of cell damage common with chemical burns. This confirms his diagnosis of a chemical burn. The question is, how did she get these burns in her bathroom? Andrews believes the chemical must be in her apartment. He suspects that it might be a cleaning product—possibly bleach—that is commonly found in homes. He asks the detectives to return to the victim's apartment to search for anything that might have caused a chemical burn, particularly bleach bottles.

The Detectives Return to the Scene

Back at the apartment, the detectives start their search in the bathroom. Andrews is right. There are two bleach bottles, one with the top on and one with the top off. Both are empty. Next, the detectives take another look at the clothes strewn around the bathroom. They are still wet, and they have the strong chemical scent of bleach.

Now Andrews knows the source of the burn. Bleach is a chemical that can be dangerous if not handled properly. But contact with skin is not the only danger. The chemical fumes bleach creates can make it hard to breathe. At least one bottle and possibly two were poured out. The fumes would have been strong enough to make the victim's eyes water and to give her trouble breathing. She may have opened the window to clear the room of fumes.

But the real damage came from contact with the bleach itself. Clearly from the burns on her body, she poured it on herself, either by accident or on purpose. The burns cover 45 percent of her body. This is a very serious injury. As Andrews points out, "your skin is [your] largest organ." The burns alone are enough to cause death. But questions remain. Why was the bathroom such a mess, with the towel rack torn down and clothes everywhere? How did the bleach end up on her skin?

The Golden Triangle of Sudden Death

In the real world of forensic medicine, cause of death is often not known until all the test results are back. On television, tests are back instantly or in hours. But for Andrews and every other forensic pathologist, it can take weeks to months for results to come back.

When the test results of the young woman return, Andrews can start to put together the facts to create the situation he believes contributed to her death. He calls the investigation process the golden triangle. "In one corner of the triangle you've got the autopsy, then at the other corners you've got the scene investigation and the medical history, and you've got to put them all together to determine the cause and manner of death."

Test Results and a Diagnosis

The toxicology test showed that there were no drugs or alcohol in the young woman's system. The eye fluid test, though, showed that her salt levels were below normal. Based on her medical history, Andrews knows that on another occasion, the student drank too much water and her salt levels became low. Possibly the same thing happened again. The changes this made in her body could have caused her to become confused and upset. She may have acted unusually then, doing things like tearing the towel rack off the wall and pouring bleach on herself.

The strong fumes probably made her rush to open the window. The fingerprints on the wall were most likely from her struggling to do this. The brown-red staining on the wall was from her skin, already showing the effects of the chemical burn. She may have suddenly realized the damage from the burn, rushing into the shower with her clothes on to try to wash off the strong chemical. Unfortunately, because of the combination of the low salt levels in her blood and the chemical burn, she collapsed and died. As the forensic pathologist, Andrews determines that the cause of death was the chemical burns, but that the low salt levels in her body contributed to the outcome.

Investigating Deaths in the Medical Examiner's Office

This case is like many forensic pathologists see, with a combination of factors leading to death. Although Andrews did not visit the location where this body was found, he does sometimes go to scenes of sudden death. This includes accidents, suicides, and homicides. In the morgue, he most often examines people who died suddenly from natural causes—meaning a medical condition caused the death.

Sometimes bodies come to the medical examiner's office unidentified. If this happens, the staff goes to great efforts to get an identification. They take note of any identifying features, such as scars and tattoos, that can help lead to an identity. Occasionally though, there are no unique marks to go by. Fingerprints and DNA are helpful only if they have someone on file to match them to.

If the medical examiner's office has an idea who the decedent may be, the staff can see if there are any dental records to compare to the decedent. Using an X-ray machine, the forensic pathologist can try to match the X-rays to dental records of missing persons. But what if the victim comes in with no teeth at all?

The next step is to check medical records. Perhaps the unidentified person had a chest X-ray taken in the recent past. If so, the staff then X-rays the victim and compares that X-ray to the one taken previously. Bones can be quite unique to each person. By comparing the chest X-rays, Andrews can sometimes determine if a missing person is in fact the decedent in the morgue.

Television, Court, and the Forensic Pathologist

Like most forensic pathologists, Andrews makes regular appearances in court to explain his autopsy findings in criminal cases. Before he begins his testimony, he is often asked to explain the limits of forensic medicine to juries. This is necessary because television gives juries unrealistic ideas and expectations of what forensic medicine can and cannot do.

Forensic TV shows often feature a forensic pathologist plunging a thermometer into a **corpse** and declaring the victim died at a specific time. In the opinion of Andrews, this kind of exact analysis for time of death is just not possible. He points out that there are too many factors to consider, all of which affect body temperature, such as where the body is found, how it is clothed, and how much it weighs. He explains: "Some pathologists will stick their neck out and say, he's been dead ten hours maybe, but I don't. When I've been asked by police or on the stand in court, I'll say any time between when he was last seen alive and when he was found dead, and that is about as accurate as I can get."

The real problem with TV forensics is that they make viewers believe that autopsies can answer every question about the cause of death. Sometimes, no reason for death is ever found. Andrews knows this can be very difficult for families to accept. "I completely understand because they want answers, and sometimes it's frustrating for me when I put out an undetermined cause of death, because I feel like I've failed. But I understand what the limitations of the autopsy are."

Forensics as a Career

In the case of a sudden death, a forensic pathologist gets to solve mysteries of medicine—and sometimes mysteries of crime, too. Sam Andrews loves his work. He describes his career this way: "I just don't know what I'm going to see every day. Some days are just routine. But some days I see some really cool stuff. And then to be able to do the autopsy—that's probably my biggest draw."

CHAPTER 3

Fighting Crime on the Fly

The corpse is a little unusual. The upper part of the body is mostly bones. The lower part is still clothed, the body inside the fabric mostly protected. This makes the corpse look long dead from the waist up, and newly dead from the waist down. The skull shows evidence of a fatal gunshot wound.

Gail Anderson is interested in all of these facts, but her examination uncovers the kind of thing that can make even experienced detectives shiver: The body is covered in masses of wriggling maggots.

When police departments across Canada are faced with maggots, blowflies, and a corpse, they ask Gail Anderson to assist with the investigation. Dead

Dr. Gail Anderson teaches forensics and forensic entomology at the School of Criminology at Simon Fraser University in Vancouver, British Columbia, Canada.

bodies, under certain conditions, attract certain insects. Anderson is an entomologist; she studies insects. She is one of the few forensic entomologists in the world. Because of her extensive knowledge about the rate at which bodies decompose and the life cycles of the insects that feed on them, she can offer the police critical information about time of death.

Forensic entomologists are often called to a crime scene if it is believed that the victim has been dead for more than 72 hours. During the first three days, the forensic pathologist can often go by the police evidence and the autopsy results to determine the time of death. After that, says Anderson, "insect evidence is often the most accurate and sometimes the only method of determining elapsed time since death."[1]

Dangers at the Scene

When Anderson arrives at the crime scene, the police protect the site until she can examine the body. The detectives give her all the information they have, and then she puts on an officer protection suit to investigate the body. This police garb protects her from accidentally having contact with anything from the crime scene, such as blood or insects. The suit also prevents cross-contamination, so that nothing on her clothes ends up on the body. Gloves add to the protection. Investigators do not know if the victim has died from a contagious disease or if the victim is infected with a disease that could pass to them. Because of this, everyone is careful about contact with bodily fluids.

Another concern is potential threats from the person who committed the crime. At the scene of a potential homicide, no one ever forgets there is still a chance that the killer may attempt to harm anyone connected with the investigation. Anderson explains, "The area is searched to check that the **perpetrator** is not nearby…. Crime scenes can be dangerous places, and everyone has to be very careful."[2]

Once she reaches the body, collecting insect evidence is Anderson's first priority. If there are maggot masses, she pulls out her thermometer to take the temperature of each group of maggots. The temperature of the maggot masses gives her valuable information to add to her investigation.

Collecting Maggots for Evidence

Next, she collects insects from different parts of the corpse, taking samples from both on and underneath the body. Forceps are used to collect insects; a

Dr. Anderson collects maggots from crime scenes. Knowing what life cycle stage the maggots are in can give Anderson a clear estimate of how long a person has been dead.

paintbrush is used to gently transfer larvae and delicate eggs into vials. Collecting the maggots, she puts half of them in a container of alcohol. The alcohol preserves them at that moment in their life cycle. She does this for two reasons. First, to correctly plot the time of death, Anderson must know the exact stage of development the insects were in when they were collected. Second, if the case goes to court, the insects preserved in alcohol will be entered as evidence.

The other half of the insects are taken to the lab to continue growing. Under carefully controlled conditions, they are raised to the adult stage of development. Some insects cannot be properly identified until they are fully grown. If the insects are large enough and far enough along in their development, then Anderson can identify what species they are.

Sometimes Anderson is accompanied to crime scenes by her students in graduate school. This gives them the chance to learn how to treat a crime scene and to learn the skills required to collect evidence. Occasionally, if the crime scene is too far away for Anderson, other people go in her place. These "identification officers" have been trained by Anderson to properly collect insect evidence when she cannot.

If different species of insects are present on the body, samples of each kind must be collected. Knowing the science of entomology is extremely important for this part of the investigation, especially if others are at the crime scene instead of Anderson. For example, if someone unthinkingly puts beetle larvae in a vial with the fly larvae, they will discover that some of the evidence has miraculously disappeared! All the fly larvae will be gone, because the beetle larvae will have eaten them. Adult beetles cannot be stored with other insects for the same reason.[3]

The final piece of evidence Anderson requires is something that cannot be seen or picked up. The weather at the scene of the crime is important because temperature affects the development rate of insects. Anderson uses a datalogger to record the weather and temperature where the body was found. She will compare this data with the data at the closest weather station.

Next, the body is placed in a body bag and taken to the morgue for an autopsy by the medical examiner. Anderson attends the autopsy to better examine the body. Often the best way to preserve evidence is to collect the body and bring it back to the morgue. If only bones remain, the body is examined right where it was found.

The Lab Work Begins

Once Anderson has collected all the evidence she needs, she returns with it to her lab at the Centre for Forensic Research at Simon Fraser University. This laboratory is different from many such labs because it has police-level security. For evidence to be used in a criminal trial, it must remain in a place where it cannot be tampered with in any way.

Back at the lab, Anderson first makes a record of

all the collected insects. Counting maggots is not for everyone, but for Anderson, it is just part of cataloging the evidence. She measures and examines each insect using a microscope.

Blowflies, Nature's Best Witnesses

Blowflies are the most common insect found on corpses in the early stages after death. These insects have an amazing sense of smell, traveling as far as several kilometers[4] to feed on animal or human flesh. Anderson says, "Certain species of insects are often the first witnesses to a crime. They usually arrive within twenty-four hours of death if the weather is suitable (i.e. spring, summer, or fall in Canada), and often arrive within minutes in the presence of blood or other bodily fluids."[5] Knowing the life cycle of the blowfly is essential for understanding how Anderson determines the time of death.

Putting the Clues Together

Anderson plots each stage of development, based on the location of the body and knowledge about the season, weather, temperature, and many other factors. These factors determine how long each life-cycle stage lasts. Putting all of the information together is complicated. Anderson's experience and research give her the tools to accurately take this

Blowflies are the insects most commonly found on corpses. This picture shows what a blowfly looks like up close.

LIFE CYCLE OF A BLOWFLY

Blowflies arrive on a body shortly after death, laying eggs in any wounds first. If no wounds are present, they do so in body openings, such as the nose, mouth, and eyes.

Each egg hatches into a first-stage maggot. This maggot feeds on the corpse and molts into a second-stage maggot.

The second-stage maggot feeds until it turns into a third-stage maggot.

When the third-stage maggot stops feeding, it moves elsewhere, usually into the clothes of the decedent or nearby soil.

The maggot unattaches from its outer layer of skin and waits until its new exterior layer turns hard. Its color changes from light to dark during this stage. After several hours, it becomes dark brown. This hard shell protects the insect as it transforms into an adult fly.

Days later, the adult fly crawls out.

The adult fly feeds and lays eggs, starting the process for the next generation of flies.[6]

information and combine it with the necessary variables to determine a time of death. She says, "What we do is interpret the evidence that is on the body, and I give a minimum time of death. So, I can say for sure this person has been dead ten days. It could be longer; it could not be less."[7]

With the case of the gunshot victim, Anderson takes all the evidence she has to determine the stage of the insects' development. One of the biggest clues? The feeding frenzy of the maggots. The temperature outside where the body was found was 15°C (59°F). Yet, says Anderson, "Even after the body was refrigerated for two hours, the temperature of the biggest maggot mass was 20°C (68°F)." The extra heat from the maggot masses speeds up their life cycle. The warmer the temperature, the faster the flies develop.

Anderson goes back to her research to plot the time of death. She calculates using the temperature of the site where the body was found and the time of year. Her research shows that it takes this kind of blowfly at least 9.3 days to reach the third stage in

WHAT ARE THE INSECTS MOST COMMONLY FOUND ON A CORPSE?

Flies and beetles. Although blowflies are most likely to land on a newly dead body, the cheese skipper arrives a while after death.[8] This small black fly is most famous for the athletic abilities of its maggots. Using their mouth hooks, they grab the center of their bodies and spring up, jumping as much as 6 inches into the air![9]

these conditions. Since the insects were collected on October 12, they must have been eggs on or before October 4. As there were open wounds on the body, and blood almost instantly brings these insects to the scene, she can conclude that the victim of this crime died on or before October 4. In the end, additional evidence from the police proved that the victim had died on October 3.

In the Courtroom

If a case goes to trial, Anderson may be called to court to explain the forensic evidence that she analyzed. She attends court as an expert witness—a specialist in her field. As a forensic scientist, her job is to show the role of entomology in determining the time of death. Anderson must explain her evidence and what her research proves about the evidence. Most importantly, she must take advanced scientific concepts and make them understandable to the judge and jury.

Lawyers will challenge her evidence, and Anderson prepares for this. This is the courtroom version of "doing your homework." She makes sure she knows all of the current information and research that might be raised about her findings. Since Anderson is constantly researching how insects can show the time of death, she refers to these studies to make her evidence strong.

Anderson's past and continuing research is the backbone of any expert testimony she gives in court. With her graduate students, she has created a large database of the appearance of insects and time of death. Such information may be critical to a trial.

Beyond Insects

As a forensic scientist, Anderson also does research beyond entomology. Sometimes Anderson investigates bodies pulled from the water. Many factors affect how bodies decompose there. Water depth and whether any of the corpse is exposed to air and insects both play a part in her analysis. Anderson's interest in entomology led her to explore the effect of other animals that feed on corpses—marine life.

Human remains are frequently found in water. Not all of them are homicides. Anyone who lives near a river, lake, or ocean knows that reports of discovered bodies are not uncommon. Accidents happen all the time through boating and swimming mishaps, including drowning. Even plane crashes sometimes occur over water. But often, if a large body of water is near a crime scene, a homicide victim has a way of ending up there.

Predicting time of death is much trickier without blowflies giving clues to when the victim died. If a corpse is submerged in water, different creatures will feed on the body. But will they scavenge the corpse predictably, the way insects do?

The VENUS Project Underwater Sea Laboratory

Anderson, who has investigated many such deaths, realized that forensic science could benefit from learning more about this subject. Not a great deal is known about the effects of decomposition in a body discovered in water. The types of creatures that feed on a body are known but not well documented. Because of this, forensic science cannot reliably pinpoint a time of death.

A new research project allows Anderson to do precisely this kind of study. VENUS, the Victoria Experimental Network Under the Sea, is a state-of-the-art underwater observatory in Victoria, British Columbia, Canada. The technology of the underwater lab provides a controlled environment from which to observe a corpse in the sea. As with many such research projects, a pig carcass (purchased from a butcher's shop) is used to stand in for a human body. The diet of the pig is similar to that of humans, so the way its body decomposes is similar, too. Even the skin of pigs is much like the skin of humans.[10]

A Pig at the Bottom of the Sea

The ROPOS ROV robot deploys the pig to the ocean floor. Above the carcass, a tripod holds a camera to take photos and video that are transmitted back to shore by a cable. Although there are lights to observe the pig, they cannot be left on because they might disturb the normal conditions of plants and animals that live near the bottom of Saanich Inlet. The lights are turned on at different times, though, so that video and digital cameras can capture the activity occurring on the pig.

The VENUS technology lets Anderson view the submerged carcass on the Internet—day or night—from her own computer. Anderson explains that she can then see what kinds of creatures feed on the pig, and also "the types of wound pattern they produce. This is also valuable when human remains are recovered, as it gives us an idea of what marks on the body

Gail Anderson with the Remotely Operated Submersible Vehicle (called ROPOS ROV) VENUS used to deploy and film the decomposition of the pig underwater.

may relate to **anthropophagy** [feeding on the body] and what may relate to the homicide."[11]

Within minutes of being on the seafloor of Saanich Inlet, the pig carcass has attracted scavenging creatures. Crabs, anemones, and lobsters are among

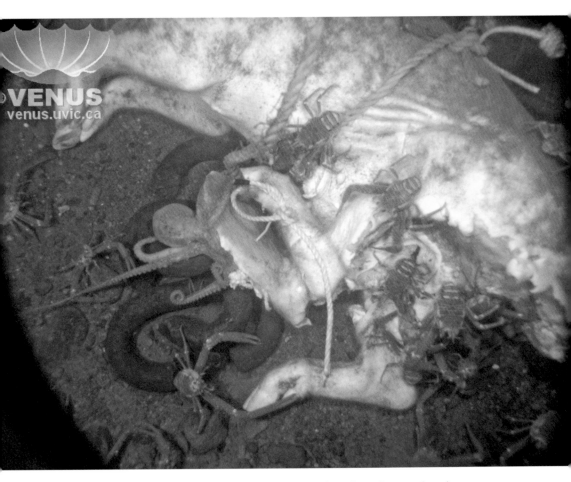

The pig carcass at the bottom of the Saanich Inlet gives scientists a better idea of what types of scavenging animals feed on remains, and how quickly.

the first. Turning on the light on the third morning reveals that something large, probably a shark, has taken a bite out of the haunches of the pig. After this happened, Anderson says, "scavengers concentrated on the hindquarters."[12] The shark bite draws sea creatures to it the same way that blowflies are attracted to a bloody wound on a body on land. A small octopus and shrimp join the feeding as well. After three weeks, most of the pig is stripped to the bone.

More work is needed to completely understand the findings of this experiment. But already it has provided information that can be used later to interpret what sea creatures might feed on a human corpse, and the signs of damage they cause. Documenting the findings will make it easier for Anderson to scientifically prove what damage comes from sea creatures, and what might be the result of a homicide. Any extra evidence leads to a clearer understanding about time of death. Gail Anderson's work is important research that will one day help convict more criminals hoping to get away with murder.

CHAPTER 4

The Mystery of the Headless Walruses

In the summer of 1992, more than five hundred dead walruses washed ashore on several beaches on the coast of Alaska. Agent Al Crane of the U.S. Fish and Wildlife Service (FWS) examines the evidence and knows he has a case on his hands that requires extra help—forensic help, in fact. It is as if the Legend of Sleepy Hollow has

Dr. Ed Espinoza is the deputy director of the U.S. Fish and Wildlife Service Forensics Laboratory in Ashland, Oregon.

invaded the quiet world of the Alaskan wilderness. Like the frightening horseman, all the walruses are headless.

The team from the U.S. Fish and Wildlife Service Forensics Laboratory in Oregon are called in to help with the case. This is the largest laboratory for analyzing animal forensic cases in the world. One of the scientists sent to investigate the headless walruses is forensic chemist Ed Espinoza.

Headhunting

Why were the walruses killed? Probably for their huge ivory tusks. The sale of illegal ivory from animals is a problem worldwide. The price their tusks can bring when sold illegally is high. The fact that these walruses are missing their heads, but have had no meat removed, indicates that they were slaughtered solely for their tusks. Scientists refer to this as headhunting, since only the head is taken, and the meat and other useful parts are left behind.

Investigating the Slaughter

The investigation into the dead walruses begins on the Seward Peninsula of Alaska. This peninsula is located on the Bering Sea. It was once part of the Bering land bridge, a tract of land that connected Russia to North America. Today, the Bering Strait separates the two landmasses by about 55 miles.[1] This relatively short distance between the two countries comes to matter during the course of this case.

As the beaches of Seward Peninsula are remote, flying in by small plane is the only way to reach the walrus carcasses. With beaches acting as runways, Espinoza and other members of the team fly to the different locations along the coast, where the animals

Walrus tusks are made of ivory, which can be sold illegally at high prices. Ivory is often carved into shapes, like the items seen here.

are rotting on the shore. They examine each dead, headless, and very smelly walrus. Espinoza pays close attention to the cut site on the neck. The exposed bones are bright white. To record this evidence, each animal is photographed, and the details are documented in notes.

While the team gathers evidence, they also take time to speak to members of the local native communities. Two main groups reside in this part of Alaska: the Inupiat and the Yupik. As a means of preserving their traditional culture, these groups are permitted to hunt walruses, as long as they harvest the meat. This is called **subsistence hunting**. If a walrus is killed, but no meat is taken, it becomes a federal offense called wasteful subsistence hunting. The native groups say they did not break the law. They suggest that the slaughter occurred in Russia, and that the ocean currents made the corpses land on the Seward Peninsula.

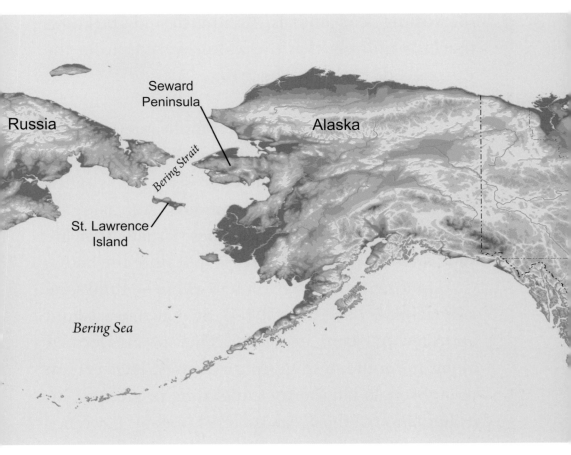

The headless walrus carcasses were found on the beaches of the Seward Peninsula, separated from Russia by only about 55 miles of water.

Following the Watery Trail

Espinoza and his team then need to find out if dead walruses can float from Russia to Alaska. With fast-moving water and the short distance between the two locations, it seems possible. Espinoza researches the way ocean currents move, and the probable path of the floating dead animals. After much study, he knows that it is unlikely that the walruses came from the Russian side of the Bering Strait.

The origin of the carcasses is still unknown. The method used to hunt walruses complicates this problem. Native hunters are allowed to kill walruses if they spot them swimming in the open sea—this is called **pelagic hunting**. More commonly, walruses are hunted when they are on **ice floes**. Usually they are shot, and then the meat is harvested from the body.

Espinoza shifts his research to where he thinks the animals may have been killed. St. Lawrence Island and Gamble Island are nearby. They are also located along the route of migrating walruses. Hunters are more likely to kill walruses migrating in groups.[2] An examination of the ocean currents from St. Lawrence Island and Gamble Island shows that dead walruses would float from there to the Seward Peninsula beaches.

Since the beaches of Seward Peninsula are remote, scientists had to travel by small planes to examine the walrus corpses.

Dead in the Water?

Once the Inupiat and Yupik are confronted with the evidence of the floating carcasses, they change their story. Yes, the native people admit, they cut the heads from the walruses. But, they say, the animals were dead when they beached on Seward Peninsula. If so, then removing their heads is not a crime.

To prove or disprove the natives' claims, Espinoza needs a way to discover if the walruses were dead when they washed up onto the beach. Espinoza believes that the animals were killed by the hunters out at sea, the heads were removed for the ivory tusks, and then the dead bodies eventually washed ashore.

Dr. Espinoza examines a walrus carcass. He is holding a numbered card to help identify the carcass when reviewing photos like this one later.

Scavengers Provide an Important Clue

It is a fact of nature that some animals gain life by feeding on the remains of dead ones. Usually, some life-form, whether microscopic or the size of a bear, will eat a carcass that is exposed on land or in water. Espinoza notes that the open neck areas on the walruses show more **predation** than the rest of the carcasses.[3] Scavengers are more likely to feed on a new or open wound.

Although the walrus is a huge animal, removing the head can be a swift process if done with a sharp knife and knowledge of walrus anatomy. The skullcap of a walrus extends farther down its back than that of most mammals. To remove the head, the neck must be cut low on the shoulder area. When the head is removed, the neck bones, called cervicals, are exposed.

On these walruses, the fleshy area around the cervicals is completely eaten away, probably by sea creatures. Because of this, it is more likely that the necks of the walruses were cut out at sea, not on the beach as the native groups claim. To prove his theory, Espinoza needs evidence.

Cow Bones for Research

To test his idea, a new research project is launched by Espinoza and his team. They position cow parts in three types of locations: the beach; onshore where the bones will be exposed to air, but occasionally washed by waves; and in the deep ocean. Over the following weeks, they evaluate the cow parts. Those in the dry or alternatingly wet and dry locations still have tissue on them and are stained with blood. The stains indicate that scavenging is recent.

The cow parts left in the underwater location are different. All of the tissue is gone, and the bones are white, without stains. This shows that the scavengers probably arrived at the site shortly after the parts were positioned. The whiteness of the bones is familiar to Espinoza: This is exactly the way the walrus cervicals looked when the carcasses were found on the beach.

Over four years of testing, the cow parts show that the bones left underwater are picked clean by fish and **arthropod** activity. This proves that the claims of the native group are untrue. The hunters killed the walruses out at sea or on ice floes, then dumped the bodies, which floated to the beaches of Seward Peninsula.[4]

A New Twist

The U.S. Fish and Wildlife Service Forensics Laboratory make their findings known around the Seward area. They hope this will stop the illegal headhunting of walruses. But the motivation to make money from the valuable ivory tusks sparks a new method to hunt without getting caught.

More walrus carcasses appear on the beach—headless, but with big slits down their bellies. Espinoza understands the idea behind the new plan: The hunters are trying to get the evidence to sink. Decay creates a great deal of gas within a carcass, making it float. By cutting the bellies, the hunters hope the walruses will sink instead of floating to shore. But because the fat layer of this animal is so thick, the gas cannot escape. Eventually the hunters realize that they cannot prevent the evidence of their crime from floating to land. Soon, in this remote area of Alaska, word spreads that nothing the hunters do can escape the eyes—and science—of the authorities.

The research activities of the Fish and Wildlife laboratory make a huge difference. The very presence of Espinoza and the others, flying up and down the coast collecting evidence, discourages hunters. In three years, the rate of wasteful subsistence hunting dropped from 84 percent to 23 percent.[5]

Dangers on the Job

Researching a crime in a remote location can be difficult work. It is not like working in a city, where help is close at hand. In 1993, during Espinoza's last year of research in Alaska, the unthinkable happened. Espinoza and a pilot were documenting walrus carcasses by flying to various locations on the shoreline, using the sandy beaches as runways. Strong winds during landings are one of the most difficult aspects of flying. In a small plane, the challenge can be even more pronounced. Along the Seward

Peninsula, the offshore winds are violent and come in powerful gusts. One day while landing, a gust hit the plane, tipping it into the ocean. Espinoza and the pilot did not panic, but quickly kicked out the windows of the sinking plane. As the aircraft went under completely, they swam through the frigid water to the beach.

They escaped one danger to face another. Being cold and wet on a beach in Alaska requires instant, common-sense decisions. Espinoza and the pilot know the dangers of **hypothermia**, when the body's core temperature goes too low. Fortunately, they had a lighter with them. The beach was covered with dry driftwood, which provided plenty of fuel to burn. A search of their pockets revealed a little bit of food between them, so they were grateful—the situation could have been far worse. They dried off and tried to get comfortable by the fire, realizing they could be in for a long wait before help arrived.

Twenty-four hours later, a rescue plane flew over them, a most welcome sight. After it landed, Espinoza and the pilot climbed onboard. Once they were strapped in, the rescue plane rolled down the sandy beach, picking up speed. Suddenly, the soft sand gave way, and the plane did a nosedive. "Then four of us had to be rescued instead of two," said Espinoza, downplaying the adventure. But this experience emphasizes that the pursuit of forensic science can sometimes have its risks.

The FWS Forensics Lab

Back at work, Espinoza acts as the Deputy Director of the U.S. Fish and Wildlife Service Forensics Laboratory. Crimes against wildlife can take many forms. Sometimes animals are hunted illegally, like the walruses in Alaska. Endangered animals are often the victims of crime, their body parts sold illegally or used in the manufacture of other products. Fish and Wildlife agents will sometimes send the lab a sample of a powder used in Asian medicine, and the staff will identify whether an endangered animal was used in its production.

The forensic lab specialists use science to help catch suspects that harm animals in less obvious ways, too—such as poisoning them with pesticides. But the challenges for the scientists are daunting at times. Often, only small body parts are recovered. Agents bring them to the lab so that someone can identify the animal species. In a human crime lab, the corpse is always *human*. In the FWS crime lab, the only evidence might be part of a feather or a piece of skin. The scientists might investigate something as small as blood droplets—but from what? They could come from *any* animal, from a bird to a lion! The next step would be to determine what *kind* of bird or lion. Espinoza says both animal and human crime labs do have something in common regarding evidence: "They all seek to ask the same question: What is it?"

New Frontiers in Forensics

As well as supervising a large staff, Espinoza ensures that any cases from the lab that go to court meet all legal rules. This can be difficult because sometimes the scientists need to prove that a crime was committed when there are no known tests to prove it. Scientists are often involved in developing new tests to prove that crimes have been committed against animals. It can be a challenge to convince a judge and jury that newly developed scientific testing is valid. If a case goes to trial, Espinoza has to ensure that the science behind the tests is solid and that no other research can challenge their results.

Chemistry in Action

The research done by Espinoza grows naturally out of the cases the lab is investigating. For example, a case is brought to the attention of Espinoza concerning the sale of guitar picks. The question is, are the picks made from plastic or from the shells of endangered sea turtles? Espinoza draws on his background as an analytical chemist. He analyzes a plastic pick so that he can re-create it in the lab. The pick is made from a protein called casein. By testing for casein, scientists in the lab can now tell the difference between the legal plastic guitar picks and the illegal ones from sea turtles. Those responsible for profiting from the death of an endangered animal can be prosecuted.

In developing a procedure or test, Espinoza follows the same rules for science that students use across country in their own science classes. A hypothesis is created, then tested and retested. As well, the procedure and test must be acceptable to other scientists who look at his data. And sometimes, despite a great deal of time and effort trying to prove a hypothesis, no definite conclusion can be reached.

A Career in Animal Forensic Science

Espinoza often meets students who are interested in becoming forensic scientists. He believes a student with an analytical mind may do well pursuing

INSIDE THE FWS FORENSICS LAB

Usually, cases are brought to the forensics crime lab by law enforcement agents, most often from the Fish and Wildlife Service. Espinoza describes his workplace as "the only full-service lab for animals," because it has all the high-tech features of a human forensics crime lab, plus everything required to deal with animal cases, too. Each person gets to handle a case based on his or her specialties within the lab.

✔ The Chemistry Unit uses chemistry and instruments to test evidence, particularly related to pesticides, poisons, and unknown materials. It also does species identification and analyzes Asian medicinal products, which are often made from endangered species.

✔ The Criminalists Unit is composed of three sections: the criminalist experts, the firearms experts, and the fingerprint experts. They examine evidence related to their specialties and also perform other laboratory tests, such as fabric identification and soil analyses.

✔ The Genetics Unit analyzes blood and tissue samples for DNA to identify animal species involved in a crime.

✔ The Morphology Unit analyzes body parts to identify what species they belong to. The unit is divided into three specialties of study: birds, reptiles, and mammals.

✔ The Pathology Unit does animal autopsies, investigating for evidence and cause of death.

✔ The Digital Evidence Unit analyzes evidence collected by cameras, audio recorders, and computers.[6]

The laboratory working as a total unit allows these scientists to save animals and be on the leading edge of forensic animal science around the world. As Espinoza says, "One piece of lab work does not solve a crime. It is always a group effort."

forensic science. Do you like puzzles? Are you a good problem-solver? Are you good at math? Then the analytical side of forensics could be for you.

Espinoza enjoys his work, but notes that it is not for everyone. Analytical chemists often work alone. If you prefer to work in groups, then this career may not be the best choice. He also does not want anyone to forget that becoming a scientist is a lot of work. But if students are prepared to work hard, a positive attitude can result in some amazing accomplishments in a forensic science career.

Even after many years in the field, the process of discovery still fascinates him. Espinoza says he is happy "when I'm working on an analytical problem and I find a solution. Usually I am alone, running samples, doing data set analysis, and can conclude things." The best part of his job? "Finding a scientific phenomenon that has never been described before." And in so doing, Espinoza uses forensic science to solve crimes against animals forced into an uneven battle for survival.

CHAPTER 5

Dinosaurs and High-Heeled Shoes

The lab is cool, and the lights are bright. Throughout the large classroom are several gurneys holding dead bodies. Clustered around the gurneys are 115 university students, who carefully remove the plastic sheets that cover the corpses.

Elizabeth Rega watches the reactions of her students. For most of them, it is their first time seeing a dead body. Walking around the lab, she instructs the students in this unusual classroom.

The students form groups, then cut or dissect the corpses as Rega advises them. The chemical smell is strong, but it effectively hides the scent of the corpses.

Dr. Elizabeth Rega teaches human anatomy and musculoskeletal biology at the School of Osteopathic Medicine at Western University in Pomona, California.

Gross (large) anatomy is a required course for all students in medical school. If they are to become doctors, students must see the body from the inside out and three-dimensionally. By dissecting dead bodies donated to medical schools, students learn how body systems work.

Rega is an expert on muscles, bones, and the conditions and diseases that attack them. She pauses at the end of one gurney, stopping to take a better look at the feet of the **cadaver** of an old woman. Rega takes out her camera. Who would think that an old woman and dinosaurs, millions of years apart, would share something in common?

Elizabeth Rega is a physical anthropologist. Anthropology is the study of human societies. A physical anthropologist studies how life in a society affects the human body. Rega describes physical anthropology as "the use of skeletal biology to find clues to the past; a kind of CSI for ancient humans and animals."[1] How she applies this knowledge to scientific mysteries is amazing.

Studying Dinosaurs

Rega studies more than just humans. She is also an expert in **paleopathology**. This branch of science is the study of diseases and injuries found in fossils. Rega says of her work: "Paleopathology is like being a medical examiner, except that all the soft tissue is missing, the animals or people are thousands to millions of years dead, and the questions you are answering concern evolution, not crime. It's like being an evo-

This is what scientists believe *Chasmosaurus* looked like.

lutionary detective." Rega applies her knowledge of skeletal systems and their diseases to dinosaurs. And that is why she is photographing the feet of an elderly woman in her gross anatomy lab.

Rega is asked to examine the hands, or **manus**, from two *Chasmosaurus* dinosaurs from the Canadian Museum of Nature. One of the hands was not recovered, but paleontologist Rob Holmes shows the remaining three to Rega. He hopes Rega can determine how the injuries on the hands occurred.

An Unlikely Dinosaur Coincidence

The anthropologist examines the bones closely. The fingers on the manus are normal. The bones are mostly smooth, other than cracks that resulted from being buried for millions of years. Strangely enough, though, all three fossil thumbs are deformed. Was this caused by an accident or illness? Rega looks at the three fossil manus sitting on her lab desk. The scientist knows that very few chasmosaur fossil hands have been found. Yet she has three hands and all have an injury in the same spot. The chance of two dinosaurs having the same injury is unlikely.

Rega reviews what she knows about these particular chasmosaur specimens. They were heavy animals, and they were old. She can see that the thumb bones grew unevenly as they tried to heal. The injury caused inflammation on the bone, and then infection. Rega believes the infection in the dinosaurs was probably bacterial or from a fungus. It would have been a **chronic condition**, meaning the dinosaurs had it for a long time, or it kept recurring. Dinosaurs lived pretty simple lives. Could the damage to the thumbs have been caused just by walking?

The Human Connection

Back at her office, the photographs of the human cadaver provide Rega with the example she is seeking. Hints of the woman's age and lifestyle are visible on her feet. **Calluses** and curved toenails indicate that for much of her life the woman wore shoes that did not fit properly. And although millions of years and evolution separate a dead woman from a dinosaur,

This is one of the *Chasmosaurus* hands Rega was asked to examine.

walking is something that caused them pain—because they both suffered from **bunions**. This is a common condition in humans, caused most often by a structural problem with the foot. Wearing shoes that are too small or high heels can also cause bunions or make them worse.[2]

Bunions become more common as people get older. The pressure of simply walking can cause them to occur. The problem does not start in the bones, though. The tissue that connects one bone to another to form a joint is called a ligament, and as people age, the **ligaments** move. When they do, the big toe bones twist inward. At the same time, the condition produces a bony growth on the joint of the big toe. It is painful—and 72 million years ago, was apparently endured even by dinosaurs!

Seeking Evidence for the Hand Injury

While there may be calluses to show that the old woman wore high heels when she was alive, there is no soft tissue left on the dinosaur fossils. This is not a criminal case, but in science, it is not enough to just state that the chasmosaurs could not walk properly. Rega needs evidence to explain why the dinosaur thumbs are deformed, because healthy animals are able to walk without hurting themselves.

The next step in her investigation is to consult again with Rob Holmes. She needs more information about how chasmosaurs walked. Rega and Holmes look at research on trackways made by similar dinosaurs. From these footprints, scientists can measure the length of dinosaur steps and see how the fingers and toes landed on the ground.

Trackways are useful, but they are only a starting point. To re-create the scene of the "crime" or the injury, Rega and Holmes must see how the chasmosaur really walked. How is this possible when the chasmosaur died millions of years ago? They use the forensic evidence they have—the dinosaur bones and the trackway.

The Chasmosaur Goes Digital

Holmes measures the dinosaur bones and creates a small model of the chasmosaur. The legs and feet are positioned to fit to the footprints of the similarly shrunken trackway pattern. Every step of the walking process is photographed. The data is entered into a computer by Alex Tirabosso, the computer animator at the Canadian Museum of Nature. The result is a digital chasmosaur walking across the computer screen![3]

Rega and Holmes can see that the dinosaur walked with a rolling, side-to-side motion. Walking this way made the chasmosaur shift its weight, putting pressure on its hands and feet.[4] As these were heavy animals, this **gait** may have contributed to the damage on their thumbs.

After reviewing all the evidence of this case, Rega understands how the injuries must have happened. The chasmosaurs suffered the effects of age, weight, and the way they walked. Whether on human feet or dinosaur hands, this condition had the same effect— bunions—without the high heels.

The Case of the Beat-up *T. rex*

The *Tyrannosaurus rex* named Sue is one of the world's most famous dinosaurs. Sue is unique because so much of her skeleton was found. An almost complete dinosaur skeleton gives researchers a far better chance for understanding the kind of life the dinosaur lived 67 million years ago.

As scientists began preparing the bones of this *T. rex*, one thing was clear: This was a huge animal, forty-two feet long and thirteen feet tall at the hips.[5] New research pegged Sue at about twenty-eight years old. In the lifetime of a meat-eating dinosaur, Sue was just about as old as such a dinosaur might get.[6]

Bumps, Breaks, Cracks, Dents and Holes

Most of Sue's bones are so well preserved that it is possible to see where the muscles attached to bones when Sue was alive. This very detail provided several mysteries for the scientist studying Sue, paleontologist Chris Brochu. His examination finds several strange bumps, holes, and growths on the *T. rex* bones. Did these injuries cause Sue's death?

Enter Rega, with her brand of dinosaur CSI. An examination of the bones reveals the forensic mysteries to Rega. Several different bones showed signs of abnormalities.

A Bad Leg Is Bad News for a *T. rex*

The first abnormality is on the lower leg bone, called the fibula. Rega examines the bone carefully. On top is extra growth that looks like a sponge. It shows that something was wrong with the fibula when Sue was alive. There is only skin protecting this bone. Because of this, any injury to the fibula could be serious. If the bone heals, the healing process itself shows.

Rega wonders if the bone was broken, as this might explain the spongy growth. The fibula is CT scanned, and this shows that the bone was not broken. There is extra bone growth in one spot, where healthy new bone formed over dead tissue. This shows something specific, a disease called **osteomyelitis**. Usually this is found after a **trauma** to the bone. Infection follows, and healing takes a long time. Rega says that with Sue's injury the healing of the bone tissue took "months to years."[7]

Some animals might not have recovered from such a serious leg wound, but Sue was lucky. The other lower leg bone, the tibia, was not affected. The tibia is the stronger of the two lower leg bones. Because only the weaker bone was affected, Sue was probably not even disabled by this significant wound.[8] The forensic evidence is clear: The wound healed, so it did not kill Sue.

Was Sue Accident-Prone?

Rega examines several other injuries on the skeleton. Two spots show injuries and bone overgrowth from healing. On the first, on Sue's back, two vertebrae are actually fused together from this kind of healing. On the second, on the tail, there was so much overgrowth that it crowded and left an imprint of the muscle on the bone!

More signs of Sue's rough life appear as Rega feels a smooth hole on the dinosaur's arm and a smaller one on the shoulder blade. Her examination of the arm shows that the bone was not broken. The holes are probably signs of pockets of infection. Sue may have received a blow in that spot, or she was hurt in a fall. It's hard to imagine a huge dinosaur with pulled muscles and ligaments, but Rega says that would have occurred with such an injury. Because the arm and shoulder are so well healed, the trauma must have occurred early in the dinosaur's life.

Hinged Ribs

The next abnormality is several cracked ribs. Oddly enough, the bone overgrowth forms a line across the

This photo shows the trauma to one of Sue's ribs.

side of Sue's body. This suggests that all the ribs suffered a trauma at the same time. The site shows a
unique healing pattern Rega recognizes from birds
and mammals. First, blood gathers around the injury.
The tissue thickens, then bone grows over the break.
This tells Rega that Sue had healthy healing on the
ribs. The scientist notes another factor: One of
the ribs has a split in the middle, almost like a hinge.
Rega knows this can occur if the bone continues to
move during healing. Considering the location of the
ribs, the bone may have kept moving simply because
of Sue's normal breathing.

Was Sue the Victim of Face Biting?

Of all the abnormalities on the *T. rex*, scientists are most interested in the damage on Sue's skull. Along the dinosaur's lower jaw is a series of holes. Are they bite marks? Was Sue once involved in a battle with another dinosaur?

There is skeletal evidence that face biting existed within the dinosaur world. When one animal bites another, the teeth leave a pattern, both side to side and up and down as the upper and lower jaws apply biting force. Face biting in dinosaurs took two forms. The first kind occurred when dinosaurs of different species fought each other. The second kind occurred when two dinosaurs of the same species competed for mates, prey, or territory.

Meat-eating dinosaurs were not known for their good manners. They roughly tore the flesh off their prey, dragging their teeth over muscle and bone. Millions of years later, those raking marks remain visible on fossils. If you bite into an apple without withdrawing any of the flesh, your teeth will leave a neat pattern. But if the apple is hanging off a string when you bite it, your teeth may leave a raking pattern instead. It is harder to bite a moving object!

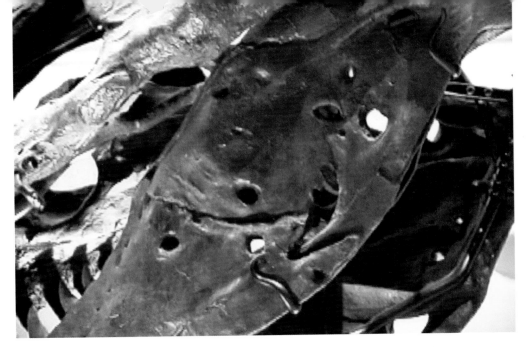

Dr. Rega believes that the holes in Sue's jaw bone were not due to face-biting, but to an illness.

Face biting seems to be the logical explanation for the holes on Sue's face. Rega, however, finds several clues that seem to disprove this theory. First, she notes that the holes do not have a jaw bite pattern. Second, she can see that the holes healed at different times. This indicates that whatever formed them did not occur all at once. Third, the holes are in a place where it would be hard to bite a dinosaur—at the back of the lower jaw, almost into the neck. Finally, similar holes exist in almost every "old" *T. rex* that has been found, as well as in other meat-eating dinosaurs.

These factors lead Rega to believe that the holes are the result of an illness that Sue lived with for a very long time. It may have been caused by bacteria or a fungus. Mouths usually contain such things, but in a healthy balance. If one kind of bacterium or fungus grew in excess, then it may have been enough to cause damage. Probably the infection started with sores, and then progressed to eating right into the jawbone, eventually leaving its "evidence" in the form of holes. Rega states that it is possible that whatever caused this illness may not even exist now.

Adding Up the Forensic Facts

There is no way to be certain that diseases that existed millions of years ago were similar to ones animals experience today. But with animals, bones are bones. Even though dinosaurs lived so long ago, and seem so different from humans, there is still a great deal of similarity in the way they healed from disease or trauma.

After examining the evidence from the *T. rex* autopsy, Rega is willing to make an educated forensic guess about how these injuries played into the death of Sue. Her conclusion? The reason for death is not evident on the skeleton. There are plenty of injuries and infection damage visible on the bones of this old dinosaur, but they all happened at different times, and all were healing or had healed. Sue's skeleton held the clues to a rough life, tangled with accidents and illness, but these events were not the cause of her death. Instead, says Rega, "Sue was a healthy animal dealing with life's insults."[9] Just as the world of human forensic science cannot always find a satisfying answer, Sue's cause of death remains a mystery.

Paleopathology—The Old and New Frontier

Paleopathology is a relatively new field in forensic science. For scientists like Rega, this field is a challenge because it is not always easy to figure out what diseases and types of healing happened in animals that are extinct. As well, it is still quite rare to discover fossils with abnormalities. The more these unusual finds are made and studied, the more we will understand about ancient injuries and illness. Fortunately for paleontologists, Rega's background in physical anthropology and skeletal biology are a perfect match to help discover the past lives—and mishaps—of dinosaurs.

Rega finds her career in paleopathology rewarding. She explains, "I was excited to use the opportunity to do good science in the field," because as a physical anthropologist she can provide different ideas to explain how injuries and diseases appear in fossils. But her work on dinosaurs offers something more. Rega says it is "a new line of evidence to understand evolution and behavior."[10] Discovering new scientific facts is fascinating work, and one where forensic CSI can go back in time, even millions of years, to solve a case.

CHAPTER 6

The Mystery of the Hidden Identity

Alison Galloway is on her way home after testifying in a homicide trial when she receives the call. Human remains were discovered in the Santa Cruz mountains of California. A steam train regularly travels through this area, and workers near the tracks uncovered human remains in possibly suspicious circumstances. Most notably, they

Dr. Alison Galloway teaches physical anthropology, osteology, and forensic anthropology at the University of Southern California, Santa Cruz.

spotted a hole in the skull. Galloway makes a detour to join the coroners and sheriff where the body was found.

Galloway is a forensic anthropologist, and human bones are her specialty. Accustomed to crime scenes, she surveys the scene before her eyes settle on the body itself. There is no soft tissue left on the skeleton. The bones have traces of roots and fungus on them, hinting that the body has been there for many years.

Galloway describes the scene. "The body was laid out on its back, the skull rolled a bit to one side as if someone had picked it up. As the leaf cover was cleared away, items were also found. These included a toothbrush, a comb, a whiskey bottle, a gold pocket watch, and a revolver with a spent bullet. It was very apparent that the person had been there a long time."[1] All of these objects are very old. The items might be valuable clues to solve the mystery of when this person died, and how.

Fascinating Clues

Before the body can be moved, Galloway must document the way it was found. She clears away all the debris, then photographs and makes a sketch of how the body lies on the ground. All known details are written down in a report.

One of the first things that interests Galloway is the presence of several coins found with the body. The newest ones are dated 1892, so the body has probably been there since at least that time. Because the remains were exposed for over 100 years, Galloway is surprised they are in such good condition.

Sometimes first impressions are valuable, so Galloway considers how this individual may have died based on the evidence right in front of her. The whiskey bottle provides one possible explanation. Did this person have too much to drink? If so, he or she could have lain down on the forest floor, not noticing that it was too cold or hot.

Despite the concerns of the workers who found the body, Galloway does not see anything unusual about the skull. She will examine it more closely once the remains are moved to her laboratory. For now, nothing in the evidence suggests an obvious cause of death. One thing catches her eye, though. At some point in the victim's life, he or she suffered a broken leg. The bones show that it healed very well.

The body is transported to the morgue for the pathologist or medical examiner's examination. Once that is done, it can be transported to Galloway's lab. There, graduate student researchers help her prepare the body for study.

Cleaning the Bones

The first thing they do is clean the bones. If there is any flesh left on the skeleton, it must be cut and removed. Since all flesh cannot be removed by this method, they must boil the bones until they are clean enough to show damage, which is "generally a very messy and smelly process." Once the bones are boiled, they use forceps, scissors and scalpels to remove any flesh that remains.

Dr. Galloway examines bones in her lab.

Luckily in this case, the bones do not have any flesh remaining. All Galloway needs to do is brush off the dirt and leaves. Next, the bones are laid out and organized as they would have been in life. Fortunately, many of the bones were recovered. Students count them to see which bones are present and which ones are missing.

Galloway's expertise in physical anthropology is helpful for the next step in forensic analysis, called the "biological profile." This part of the examination will help identify the body.

Usually Galloway begins by determining if the skeleton is male or female. To do this, she also considers the evidence with the body, where it was found, and the habits of people a hundred years ago. Since the body was found in the woods with a whiskey bottle, a gun, and coins, this hints more at a man's activities than a woman's.

A Surprising Discovery

Next, the team takes measurements of the various bones. For the long bones, a bone board is used. It has a sliding scale to measure the sizes of the bones. Calipers, a set of arms that open and close, are used to measure bones as well.

Galloway explains her findings from the skeleton: "The circumstances of this case strongly suggested male, but when we looked at the bones we were surprised to find that many of the features we use to determine sex were actually female. The best area to determine sex is the front of the pelvis, but that was missing due to weathering of the bone. The back part of the pelvis had a wide notch, which we usually see in females, and the lengths of the long bones were more characteristic of female than male. The joint sizes were also not clearly male or female."

Evidence at this point leans toward identifying the victim as female. Clues from the bones also hint that the victim was of European descent. This does not necessarily mean the person came from Europe. It means that the victim came from a line of people who share characteristics of people who once lived in Europe.

Difficulties in Determining Height

Estimating the height of the person is the team's next task. Usually this is done using a formula that includes the length of the long bones and the sex of the victim. This process is made more difficult for Galloway and her students because they are still not sure if the victim was male or female. From their analysis of the bones, however, they believe that the victim's age was within the "forty- to sixty-year range" at the time of death.[2]

Next, the skeleton is examined to see if any injuries occurred at the time of death. This brings Galloway back to the skull, as workers who originally found the remains believed there was a trauma to the head. After looking at the skull, Galloway notes that there is no sign of trauma to the head. There is an opening at the base of the skull where the spinal cord passes through, and she believes this is the hole that the workers reported.

The Femur Hides a Clue

For the rest of the skeleton, the team uses a microscope to search the bones for signs of trauma or history, like past breaks and healing. Further inspection of the **femur**, or thighbone, shows that the site of the past break is smooth, meaning it healed very well. The amount of healing shows that the break occurred at least ten years before the individual died.

How did the bone become broken? There is no clue from looking at the outside of the femur, since it healed so perfectly. On a hunch, Galloway does a **radiograph** of the injury site. She is pleased to see the answer is, in fact, still inside the bone more than a hundred years later. The radiograph shows lead particles still visible in the bone. Most certainly, these came from a gunshot wound.

Conflicting Evidence

With the evidence they have, Galloway and her students cannot explain how the victim died, but the healed gunshot wound brings up the gender mystery again. This type of trauma would be far more likely to happen to a man than to a woman.

Galloway and her students stare at the skeleton on the table before them. Many of the decedent's

A COOL GADGET: THE MANDIBULOMETER

The mandible is a jawbone. This gadget is used for measuring the lower jaw; this information is added to the biological profile.

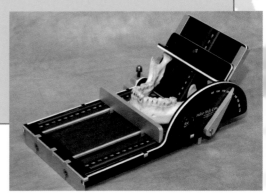

features are female. However, the healed gunshot wound, the gun, the spent bullet, the pocket watch, and the whiskey bottle are clues that suggest the victim was male. The combination of research and evidence bring up an amazing idea. Could both be right? The facts suggest that if the victim was a woman, she was most likely pretending to be a man!

There may be several reasons why a woman in the late nineteenth century would choose to live as a man. Scientists can only make conclusions based on the evidence they have. Galloway and her students analyze everything they know about this case. The forensic anthropologist then has each person on her team go through the facts, presenting a "case" based on the evidence. This process allows each student his or her own interpretation—with the chance to defend it, too.

Galloway insists that they all agree that the analysis is correct before each team member signs his or her name to the final report. With the victim in this case, they agree there is no evidence that this individual's death was the result of a crime. The cause of death remains unknown, as does the mysterious reason this woman chose to live her life as a man.

Galloway relates that the local historical society claimed the remains, burying the body as "one of the founding fathers of the community," despite the fact that research showed that the body was female. Alison Galloway explains that her lab could have done DNA testing to confirm the gender, but instead, did not. They thought that if "she had 'passed' as a male, she could go to the grave as she had lived."

Working the Crime Scene—Not as Easy as It Looks on TV

Some crime scenes are more complicated than the mysterious "man" found near the railway tracks, particularly if the crime is recent. Experience has helped Galloway create a system to carefully examine the site and collect evidence. Usually her students accompany her. There is a lot of work to be done when recovering bodies, and all of it must be documented.

Crime scenes can be local, says Galloway. "We have had them in backyards or even under the house in a crawl space." Most often, crime scenes she is called to are in remote locations. Finding them is easier if she and her team meet the police at a prearranged place and all go together. But this is not always possible, and instructions to find crime scenes are sometimes unclear if the body is in a wilderness or unpopulated area. A further problem is that cell phones often do not work in remote places.

Crime Scene Hazards

Recovering human remains can be dirty, smelly, and sometimes dangerous work. Most often the team wears clothes that are easily washed. Sometimes they wear disposable suits. Good boots with toe protection are necessary, as the condition of the crime scene is often unknown until they get there. Galloway's team must be ready for mud or rocks and be able to get good traction in case the crime scene is on a steep hill. In such places, they sometimes string up ropes so that no one falls. Other safety concerns include avoiding poison oak and stinging nettles, as well as rattlesnakes and scorpions. Galloway's team always carries a first aid kit to help treat injuries or exposure to poisonous plants. Insect repellent is also a must.

Galloway's job is to collect the body for later analysis. Because of her expertise with skeletons, this is the kind of case on which she will typically be asked to assist, particularly if the bones are scattered. Galloway explains, "It is helpful to have an anthropologist at the scene because the bones are harder to find than expected. While just about anyone can pick out a skull, finding the wrist bones among the leaves or ribs from a pile of branches is harder."

Mapping the Crime Scene

The team makes a **grid** map of the crime scene. They use string and tape measures to lay out one marked area. Galloway and her students cross the strings to make evenly spaced squares within a larger area. A map of the grid is drawn, and bones and objects found are marked to show their exact location. This method works best if the crime scene is not too large.

More often, Galloway and her team use a total mapping station unit that produces maps on a computer. It takes longer to set up than the string method, but if the crime scene is large, such as when the remains have been scattered over a large area, it saves time in the end. Each bone or item found is listed and counted, and its location is noted on the map. Everything is photographed with a digital camera.

Buried Bodies

A buried body requires different recovery techniques. While the team may use shovels, more often they use archaeological methods to do a thorough search of the dig site. This ensures that they do not miss anything or damage the contents of the site. Galloway uses a probe or masonry trowel on the soil surface. By doing this, she can tell if the ground is solid or loose, indicating a possible grave. Galloway says that having such experience allows them to "find the edges of the grave based on the feel of the digging."

The procedure is tricky because Galloway wants to disturb the body as little as possible at first. It is important to note—and photograph—how any objects in the grave are positioned compared to the body. Once this is done, her team uses a screen to sift the dirt and catch any small bones or objects that might be important to the case. The team particularly hopes to find such items as bullets, jewelry, clothing, or identification. These things can help investigators identify the victim, and may help solve the crime.

Going to Court

Once Galloway has concluded her analysis in a crime case, she often must testify in court. This requires some preparation. Everything related to the case must be documented so that she can refer to it in court. The "chain of custody" is important. This documentation shows that the evidence—including the body—has been treated properly and securely, and has been accounted for every moment during an investigation.

For court appearances, one must be prepared in both technical and practical ways. Scientific experts are always asked about their qualifications when they testify, so Galloway brings extra copies of her report as well as a history of her academic and work history as a forensic anthropologist. Everyday matters are not forgotten either. Galloway brings extra clothes and other personal items because testifying can often take more than one day, or there can be delays while waiting to testify. Waiting is a big part of court appearances. Testifying can also be difficult because the opposing attorney will challenge Galloway's findings on a case. As the anthropologist points out, "That is their job—so the best outcome [for them] is that they get you off the stand quickly so you don't impress the jury much."

There is little doubt that the work of the forensic anthropologist often provides critical information for solving crimes. Putting the facts together, interpreting them, and finding the cause of death are major motivators for Galloway, both in her work and in her research. "Sometimes we are able to be very close to determining the actual sequence of events, and that is very encouraging."

The Satisfying Work of Forensic Anthropology

Galloway finds her work rewarding when forensic science helps identify the dead and helps bring those responsible for the death to justice. However, Galloway believes future forensic anthropologists need to recognize that this career is not the exciting one portrayed on television. "Do not expect [forensic work] to be glamorous," she warns.

While solving the mystery of a death is satisfying for Galloway, there is more to it than that. She finds it gratifying to "help someone who is now beyond help. We come to respect our subjects and want resolution for them."

These ideas have led Galloway to become involved with ethical issues about respecting the dignity of the dead in forensic science. In the case of the skeletal remains found by the railway tracks, a community came forward to bury the body. But if this is not the case, how should skeletal remains be stored? Often they are in boxes. Should something more be done to honor them? Should human remains be put on display? These are the kinds of questions she is exploring. In her own cases, she wants a respectful ending wherever possible. Whether this includes a murder conviction or returning the remains to the family, Galloway concludes, "It feels good to 'settle' them somewhere."

CHAPTER 7

Plan Ahead!

How to Prepare for a Career in Forensic Science

Is Forensic Science for You?

Do you share traits with any of the scientists profiled in this book? They all have a strong work ethic, a keen attention to detail, and a strong background in science. These are mandatory for most fields within forensic science, as is a university education that may go beyond a bachelor's degree.

Medical investigators often have a university degree or a combination of police and medical backgrounds. Criminalists are becoming more and

CAUTION   CAUTION

more specialized. The trend indicates that a solid science university degree will soon be a minimum requirement. Careers such as latent print examiners or morgue technicians require less formal education. The following sections will give you some advice from the forensic scientists you have met in this book, and also some information about jobs in their fields.

Advice from Heidi Robbins, Senior Criminalist:
"If you want to be a forensic scientist, you need to be a strong student overall, but particularly in math and science. Also, you must have a college degree for this job, so at a young age, you must prepare yourself with a school curriculum that lends itself to college or university admission. The ability to be comfortable speaking in front of people is also a desirable skill for a criminalist. Such things as the debate team or speech club could help with your public speaking skills."[1]

Advice from Dr. Sam Andrews, Forensic Pathologist:
Andrews suggests that students focus on their sciences in school, particularly biology and chemistry. He strongly believes that anyone interested in a career in medicine needs to get experience in the field. As a student, volunteering in a hospital is the best way to do this. Once in college, students should try to

Senior Criminalist	
Education Required	Minimum of bachelor of science degree. Many have a master's degree; some have a PhD.
Heidi Robbins' Education	Bachelor of science degree in biochemistry and cell biology Master's degree in criminalistics
Average Salary	$76,000–$95,000
Criminalist	
Education Required	Minimum of bachelor of science degree
Average Salary	$56,000–$69,000 (May be lower or higher depending upon location)
Forensic Identification Specialist (Latent Print Examiner)	
Education Required	Degree in police science or related field (most agencies)
Average Salary	$52,000–$66,000 (May be lower or higher depending upon location)

Forensic Pathologist	
Education Required	Bachelor of science Doctor of medicine degree (MD) 5-year residency in anatomical pathology 1-year fellowship in forensic pathology
Dr. Sam Andrews' Education	Bachelor of science in physical sciences Doctor of medicine degree (MD) 5-year residency in anatomical pathology 1-year fellowship in forensic pathology
Average Salary	$140,000–$220,000
Morgue Technician (also called Autopsy Assistant)	
Education Required	Usually some college science courses, but experience can be acceptable instead
Average Salary	$28,000–$52,000
Medical Investigator	
Education Required	Depends on medical examiner's office. Many are former registered nurses, paramedics, or police officers. Most have a bachelor's degree.
Average Salary	$20,000–$60,000

Forensic Entomologist	
Education Required	Bachelor of science degree; Master's degree; PhD
Dr. Gail Anderson's Education	Bachelor of science degree, honors in zoology Master's degree in pest management PhD in entomology
Average Salary	$50,000–$110,000 (Canada)
Identification Officer	
Education Required	Typically, must work as a police officer for at least three years, upon acceptance to become an identification officer, extensive courses, testing, and on-the-job training are required. College preferred in science and/or forensics program.
Average Salary	$33,000–$69,000 (US and Canada)
Analytical Forensic Chemist	
Education Required	Bachelor of science degree; Master's degree; PhD
Dr. Ed Espinoza's Education	Clinical chemistry/medical technology science degree Master's degree in forensic toxicology PhD in forensic chemistry
Average Salary	$35,000–$130,000 based on experience

volunteer with a physician. Students must understand that becoming a forensic pathologist will not happen overnight. "The time commitment is the biggest thing they have to realize. After high school I went to school for fourteen additional years."[2]

Advice from Dr. Gail Anderson, Forensic Entomologist:
"Get a solid science background in the area of interest, do not try to be a generalist. Do not try to leap into forensic science until you have a strong scientific background in your own science first."[3]

Advice from Dr. Ed Espinoza, Forensic Chemist:
"If kids already have an ability to be a good mathematician, biologist, or chemist, they should consider wildlife forensic science to be a way to use skills they already possess. Once they have the studies, focus on analytical skills, pursue that, then later focus on forensics. That is, be a chemist first."[4]

Advice from Dr. Elizabeth Rega, Physical Anthropologist:
"Take science classes such as evolutionary biology, anatomy, physics, and statistics. Find a researcher whose work you like and volunteer in the lab, field or museum."[5]

Advice from Dr. Alison Galloway, Forensic Anthropologist:
"I would advise junior high students to focus on their

Physical Anthropologist	
Education Required	Bachelor's degree; Master's degree; PhD
Dr. Elizabeth Rega's Education	Bachelor of arts degree in biology and German Master's degree in biological anthropology PhD in biological anthropology Being a physical anthropologist gives Dr. Rega the opportunity to use her knowledge in a completely different field. She has worked as an anatomy and movement adviser for several major animated films, including *Mulan*, *Brother Bear* and *Tarzan*.
Average Salary	$45,000–$90,000
Physical Anthropologist/Forensic Anthropologist	
Education Required	Bachelor's degree; Master's degree; PhD
Dr. Alison Galloway's Education	Bachelor of arts degree in anthropology Master's degree in forensic anthropology PhD in physical anthropology
Average Salary	Professor $50,000–$100,000 Consulting in forensics $10,000–$30,000 extra per year

science classes. They could also see if there is a crime lab in the area that allows tours and organize one. Starting in high school, they should really hit the science classes—biology, anatomy, and chemistry, in particular. Absolutely essential is keeping out of trouble!"[6]

What You Can Do Now

For students still in primary, middle, and high school, work hard at math and core sciences, like biology, chemistry, and physics. Learn about animals and keep up with changes in computer technology. Visit your local library, because reading about forensic science is something you can do today. And stay curious, because regardless of how much education is required, curiosity is perhaps the most important quality that all forensic scientists share!

UNIVERSITY DEGREES

Bachelor of Arts or Science: Earned usually after a four-year full-time college program. **Master's:** An advanced degree requiring a bachelor's degree and then usually a combination of two to four years of coursework and a thesis (a written research project).
Doctor of Philosophy (PhD): A top degree that requires a master's degree plus at least two more years of coursework in a specific field and a dissertation (a written research project) on a specialized subject within the student's previous degrees.

Chapter Notes

Chapter 1. The Calling Card Murderer

1. Heidi Robbins, personal interview, August 1, 2007. Unless otherwise indicated, all quotes from Robbins come from this interview.
2. Indianapolis–Marion County Forensic Services Agency, "Latent Print Examiner," n.d., <http://www.indygov.org/eGov/County/FSA/Disciplines/latent_examiner.htm> (October 16, 2008).

Chapter 2. The Golden Triangle

1. Sam Andrews, personal interview, April 18, 2008. All quotes from Andrews come from this interview.

Chapter 3. Fighting Crime on the Fly

1. Gail S. Anderson, "Forensic Entomology: The Use of Insects in Death Investigations," *Case Studies in Forensic Anthropology*, S. Fairgreave, editor, (Toronto: Charles C. Thomas, 1999), pp. 1–12.
2. Gail Anderson, e-mail correspondence with author, June 1, 2007. Unless otherwise indicated, all quotes from Anderson come from this e-mail.
3. Gail S. Anderson, "Forensic Entomology."
4. Gail Anderson, e-mail correspondence with author, July 22, 2008.
5. Gail S. Anderson, "Forensic Entomology."
6. Ibid.
7. Canada AM – CTV Television, Broadcast Script, Toronto, Canada, March 19, 2001.
8. Gail S. Anderson, "Forensic Entomology."
9. "The Cheese Skipper," MSN Encarta, n.d., <http://encarta.msn.com/encyclopedia_761584521/Cheese_Skipper.html> (October 16, 2008).

10. Gail Anderson, "August 2006: Forensic Investigations in the Saanich Inlet," *Research Highlights: The Venus Project*, n.d., <http://www. venus.uvic.ca/> (October 16, 2008).
11. Ibid.
12. Gail Anderson and Canadian Chemical News, "Forensics Overboard," (November/December 2006), pp. 14–15.

Chapter 4. The Mystery of the Headless Walruses

1. The National Park Service, "Bering Land Bridge National Preserve," *Prehistory of Alaska*, n.d., <http://www.nps.gov/akso/ akarc/cr_bela.htm> (October 16, 2008).
2. Alaska Department of Fish and Game, "The Walrus," December 17, 2007, <http://www.adfg.state.ak.us/pubs/ notebook/marine/ walrus.php> (October 16, 2008).
3. Edgar O. Espinoza et al., "Taphonomic Indicators Used to Infer Wasteful Subsistence Hunting in Northwest Alaska," *Anthropozoologica*, No. 25 26, 1997, pp. 103–112.
4. Ibid.
5. Ed Espinoza, telephone interview, May 16, 2007. Unless otherwise indicated, all quotes from Espinoza come from this interview.
6. U.S. Department of the Interior, "The U.S. Fish and Wildlife Service Forensics Lab," September 23, 2008, <http://www.lab.fws. gov/> (October 16, 2008).

Chapter 5. Dinosaurs and High-Heeled Shoes

1. Elizabeth Rega, e-mail correspondence with author, April 21, 2007. Unless otherwise indicated, all quotes from Rega come from this e-mail.
2. Elizabeth Rega and Robert Holmes, "Manual Pathology Indicative of Locomotor Behavior in Two Chasmosaurine Dinosaurs," *Society of Vertebrate Paleontology presentation*, October 2006.

3. Stefan Thompson and Robert Holmes, "Forelimb Stance and Step Cycle in *Chasmosaurus irvinensis*" Dinosauria: Neoceratopsia. *Palaeontologia Electronica* vol. 10, issue 1, 2007, pp. 1–17.

4. Ibid.

5. The Field Museum, "Sue's Vital Statistics," *Sue at the Field Museum*, 2007, <http://www.fieldmuseum.org/sue/about_vital .asp> (October 16, 2008).

6. Gregory M. Erickson et al., "Gigantism and Comparative Life-History Parameters of Tyrannosaurid Dinosaurs," *Nature* vol. 430, 2004, pp. 772–775.

7. Elizabeth Rega, e-mail correspondence with author, April 23, 2007.

8. Chris Brochu, "Osteology of *Tyrannosaurus rex*: Insights from a Nearly Complete Skeleton and High-Resolution Computed Tomographic Analysis of the Skull," *Memoir 7, Society of Vertebrate Paleontology*, 2003, p. 116.

9. Elizabeth Rega, e-mail correspondence with author, April 23, 2007.

10. Ibid.

Chapter 6. The Mystery of the Hidden Identity

1. Alison Galloway, e-mail correspondence with author, May 11, 2007. Unless otherwise indicated, all quotes from Galloway come from this e-mail.

2. Alison Galloway, e-mail correspondence with author, May 27, 2008.

Chapter 7. Plan Ahead!: How to Prepare for a Career in Forensic Science

1. Heidi Robbins, e-mail correspondence with author, July 30, 2007.

2. Sam Andrews, personal interview, April 18, 2008.

3. Gail Anderson, e-mail correspondence with author, June 1, 2007.

4. Ed Espinoza, telephone interview, May 16, 2007.

5. Elizabeth Rega, e-mail correspondence with author, April 23, 2007.

6. Alison Galloway, e-mail correspondence with author, May 11, 2007.

Glossary

accelerant—A substance (like gasoline) that is used to help spread a fire.

anthropophagy—Animals that eat the flesh of humans.

arson—A fire started intentionally. Committing arson is a crime.

arthropod—An animal with a hard exterior skeleton and jointed legs. This group includes crabs, centipedes, spiders, and insects.

autopsy—An examination of a corpse done to determine the cause of death, looking at both the outside and inside of a body by dissecting it.

bindle—A piece of paper folded to securely hold trace evidence. Also called a pharmaceutical fold, or druggist's fold.

biological fluids—Any fluid that comes from the body, such as saliva, sweat, blood, and urine.

bunions—A deformity caused by structural problems with the foot or by wearing shoes that are too tight.

cadaver—The dead body of a human.

callus—A thickened area of bone or tissue.

chronic condition—A condition that is continuous, or keeps returning over a long period of time.

corpse—The dead body of a human or animal.

decedent—A dead person.

decompose—To break down or decay.

DNA (deoxyribonucleic acid)—Genetic material found in the cells of organisms. It is made of two chains of nucleotides in the form of a double helix.

femur—The thighbone.

forensics—The use of science to help solve crimes and medical mysteries.

gait—The way an animal or human walks or runs.

grid—A series of perpendicular lines that intersect at regular intervals to form small squares within a larger staked area; it is used for mapping locations within crime scenes.

homicide—The killing of one human being by another.

hypothermia—Abnormally low body temperature that can cause death.

ice floes—Large flat chunks of ice that float in the ocean.

ligaments—Strong tissues that connect bones or cartilage.

lug—The raised part of a boot tread that provides extra traction.

manus—Hand.

osteomyelitis—An infection that causes an inflammation of the bone with pain, redness, and swelling.

paleopathology—The study of changes from diseases, injuries, or abnormalities in fossils.

pelagic hunting—Hunting in the open sea.

perpetrator—Someone who commits a crime.

predation—The act of one organism feeding on another, often by killing it first.

radiograph—A photograph taken using radiation such as X-rays or gamma rays.

stereomicroscope—A large microscope that can be moved at different angles to view objects too large for regular microscopes.

subsistence hunting—Hunting in which the meat is harvested.

taphonomy—The study of the processes that occur to plants and animals after death and burial, including decay and fossilization.

toxicology—The study of the effects of chemicals on the human body, particularly drugs and poisons.

trauma—An injury.

Further Reading

Books

Adams, Bradley J. *Forensic Anthropology*. New York: Chelsea House, 2007.

Friedlander, Mark P., Jr., and Terry M. Phillips. *When Objects Talk: Solving a Crime with Science*. Minneapolis, Minn.: Lerner Publications Company, 2001.

Harris, Elizabeth Snoke. *Crime Scene Science Fair Projects*. New York: Lark Books, 2006.

Hunter, William. *Solving Crimes with Physics*. Philadelphia, Pa.: Mason Crest Publishers, 2006.

Jackson, Donna M. *The Wildlife Detectives: How Forensic Scientists Fight Crimes Against Nature*. Boston: Houghton Mifflin, 2002.

Platt, Richard. *Forensics*. New York: Kingfisher Books, 2008.

Internet Addresses

The U.S. Fish and Wildlife Service Forensics Laboratory

http://www.lab.fws.gov/students.php

The VENUS Under the Sea Laboratory

http://venus.uvic.ca/

Virtual Exhibit on Forensic Science

http://www.virtualmuseum.ca/Exhibitions/Myst/en/index.html

Index